Retire Inspired!
A Mini Guide To Your Perfect Retirement

DONA DICKINSON

ISBN:
ISBN-13: 978-1-7905-2351-1

DEDICATION

Thanks to my wonderful friends and family who encourage me every day.

CONTENTS

1 INSPIRATION

When we breathe, we are "inspiring". Breathing in spirit.

After years of working, this is the time to reclaim or discover our true selves, our spirit. It is time to build a life that lets us discover ourselves and live in a new way. A life that encourages learning, growth and fun. After a year and a half of retirement, I'm finding life is full of new experiences, friends and possibilities.

Let's get started envisioning and creating your new life, and retire inspired!

2 INTRODUCTION

Welcome to retirement!

This book is designed to help you find your path in retirement, whether you've made the leap, or are preparing for your new life.

It is not a financial guide to retiring, or maintaining your finances. Please make sure you have a will and advanced medical directives. You need a financial plan. There are independent financial advisors that can help you assess and plan – they get paid by you to give advice, and are not investment brokers paid to steer you in a specific direction. I am not qualified to help with these matters, so from here out, I'll stick to the social aspects of your retirement.

This book is written assuming that you are not rolling in excess funds, or you'd be taking that around the world cruise. It is written for everyone who has spent years committed to their work, and their families, and has wondered, "What would I do with no schedule and no work companions? ".

Most of what I do in retirement is free, or low cost, and I'll present ideas for you to follow that allow for fun and growth and engagement. And don't forget to ask for the "senior discounts"!

Limited physical capacity does not end your opportunities to grow and benefit from new connections, as you'll see from the upcoming chapters.

Many of us create artificial limitations on ourselves: "I'm not the kind of person that travels", "I don't get involved in groups", "I always (name your thing)". Retirement is a great time to release the limitations that we may have put on ourselves. Explore who we really can be, and what really interests us. Try eliminating the limiting stories about yourself that you tell yourself, and see what unfolds.

We will explore some of the many ways to bring the best years of your life into being. I've divided the book into short sections packed with ideas to add enjoyment and meaning to your retirement life.

3 HOW TO USE THIS BOOK

Read through and highlight what looks interesting to you in each category.

Challenge yourself to follow up with two or three ideas to start with. You can add new things at any time, switch to new things, and release those that don't fit after you give them a fair chance.

The goal is to create a retirement that is meaningful to you, increases your health, and is custom tailored to meet your needs. You are constructing your new life – make it one you love!

I'll guide you through chapters on:

• Physical Activity

• Art

• Volunteering

• Reading and writing

• Culinary Arts

• Learning

• Games

• Friends and family

• Side businesses/Part time work

• Music

• Travel

• Spiritual growth

• Creating new routines

Please use this book as a tool to discover what you really like. You probably have additional ideas or areas you'd like to include in your post-work years. By all means, add on and enjoy yourself!

4 PHYSICAL ACTIVITY

(Please see your doctor prior to starting a new exercise routine)

One important aspect of your new life is to think about is the care of your body. Keeping in active, or becoming active, can improve your retirement years. There are many activities that can be safely started by most people, even those who are labeled "disabled".

There are specialized classes designed for seniors offered by most gyms/YMCAs/parks. Some of these courses, like the Silver Sneakers branded classes, may be covered by your health insurance plan or Medicare. Local county and city parks, churches, synagogues and temples offer classes, often at reduced rates for seniors. And assisted living locations may offer classes open to the public.

One excellent way to get moving is walking. Make sure you have comfortable, supportive shoes. If you live in an area with inclement weather, you may find "mall walking" clubs, which offer a safe and level environment, as well as companionship. Local parks may have marked trails, and often offer guided walks that include observation of birds and natural scenery. Walking outdoors, even for a relatively short duration each day can help you keep your bones strong, and keep your heart in good working order.

Tai chi, an ancient martial art, uses very slow movement and breath. It is great for seniors, improving balance and coordination, and requires no equipment – just a bit of level ground, comfortable shoes, and clothes you can move in. In addition to the many sources of classes listed earlier, local martial arts centers (Tae Kwon Do, Judo, etc.) may offer classes. There are good videos on YouTube, as well as DVDs to learn at home. Those confined to a wheelchair can also practice, arm movement and breath will help with arm strength and help keep lungs breathing well.

Dancing engages the mind and the body, and is a great addition to your activity list. Dance studios, city and county parks and dance clubs offer classes from tango to square dance to Bollywood. Learning new steps keep your memory sharp, and all dance improves balance and keeps joints mobile. And it is fun!

Swimming or water exercise classes are offered at gyms, parks, YMCAs, and community pools. Water keeps the body buoyant, and alleviates stress on the joints. It is great for letting you move comfortably. If you haven't learned to swim yet, try an adult beginner class or try a water exercise class done in only a few feet of water. This is a great way to keep active and moving if you have any restrictions in your movements. It is also very easy on the joints, so if you have joint pain, or are carrying extra pounds, water classes can let you be active and comfortable. I recently saw an aqua Zumba class offered at my gym – which is a great way to enjoy the dance moves of Zumba in a gravity-free environment.

Golf is a good way to get outside and enjoy friends. Municipal or county courses cost less than private clubs, and many offer lessons to beginners. Used equipment can be found on Craigslist, so you can try out the sport without buying high cost clubs.

Weight lifting or resistance band training are very helpful for maintaining muscle mass and strong bones. You don't need expensive equipment – dumbbells and bands are effective. You can learn safe lifting from class at a gym, rec center or you can watch DVDs or online classes. Start slowly, with light weights or bands. Scientific studies have shown that muscle strength can be improved in our nineties! Stronger muscles reduce the risk of falling, as well as improving our metabolism.

Water activities, like rowing, kayaking or canoeing, are a great way to be outdoors, strengthen our bodies, and commune with nature. Your local parks may offer inexpensive rentals of canoes, rowboats or kayaks. Many people enjoy participating in rowing teams.

Outdoor outfitters, like REI, may offer classes in your area. Stand up paddle boards are also an option, on lakes, on rivers, and even in pools. These challenge our balance and work our bodies.

Gardens bring beauty, food, and exercise

Gardening is excellent exercise, and brings the benefit of flowers or tomatoes! If you live in an apartment, your city may have community gardens that offer small plots to its citizens. You may have a friend who would welcome some extra hands in the garden. Schools, libraries and senior centers may also offer an opportunity to garden if you do not have a yard. Even in an apartment, window boxes allow a way to bring some of the outdoors in, eat some homegrown herbs, or simply enjoy the presence of plants. Many garden clubs offer a chance to get to know other gardeners, and be active in the care of a community or public garden.

Yoga improves balance and mobility, and is offered for people of all physical abilities. Look for classes or DVDs/online classes labeled "gentle yoga" or "chair yoga' or "yoga for seniors" or Silver Sneakers. If you are new to yoga, chair yoga is a good place to start. Many recreation centers, senior centers, gyms and parks offer classes designed for older beginners. These classes are performed in loose clothes (no Lycra "yoga clothes" needed, just sweatpants and T-shirt).   This ancient practice of breath and movement has been shown to improve stress levels, as well as physical mobility. My mother started yoga at 84, and loves it. Give it a try!

Carolyn was one of my yoga students. She took yoga class and Silver Sneakers classes into her mid-80s, despite carrying oxygen for emphysema. She started exercising her mid-60s, since when she grew up, girls weren't encouraged to exercise. She was active and engaged and enjoyed the companionship of her classmates. She was an inspiration to me and to her classmates, and showing us that being active and full of life can continue throughout our whole life span.

Group exercise classes, from Pilates to barre, create strong bodies and encourage joint movement. You'll get the benefit of getting to know others in your class as well as improving your health. If you want to try one, often gyms/fitness clubs/Pilates studios will allow you to try one class for free without a commitment.

Senior teams for men and women for softball, bowling, soccer, crew (rowing), or kickball offer a chance to bond with others and get your exercise.

Exercise is the best medicine available, reducing risk of falls, improving health and enhancing mood. Give yourself the gift of an active, long life by finding your physical activity.

The best one to choose is the one that you will do!

Time for you to learn to ride?

5 ART

Many of us enjoyed making some kind of art as children or young people, and somehow lost that connection to our inner artist.

There are a wide variety of arts to learn and engage with. Find one you like, and stick a toe in. Then, try another. See what activity is fun for you. Release expectations of a specific outcome and enjoy the journey. Experiment to see which is pleasurable. Many art forms, like watercolor, start with a small and inexpensive kit – pencil, watercolors, brushes and paper. No need to buy extensive materials to try out new art.

For activities that require tools, look into tool sharing sites, or craft store classes or a group to see if you enjoy the art without investing in equipment you may not want. Enjoy the process of creating. Practice will improve results, and we can enjoy the process from our first artistic project!

Once you start looking, you will find many sources of learning about a new art form. For example, I am using a book to learn how to watercolor. I practice each exercise several times, and enjoy seeing the progress as I work on the pictures. This is an inexpensive way to learn, and is accessible to almost everyone.

Here are a few options to consider:

• Pottery	• Quilting
• Watercolor or oils or pastels	• Basket weaving

- Drawing
- Sculpting
- Jewelry making
- Carpentry
- Glass making
- Stitchery
- Furniture building
- Crochet
- Coloring (pencil or crayon)
- Hat making
- Stained glass
- Paper making
- Collage
- Photography
- Book making
- Sewing
- Knitting
- Whittling
- Candle making
- Birdhouse building
- Mosaics
- Macramé

There are a wide variety of artists who demonstrate techniques and ideas on online media. For instance, searching for "how to make a birdhouse" brings up videos as well as books and plans. Wikihow.com is a great place to start looking for information and ideas.

If your city or county has a parks program, often inexpensive classes in a variety of arts are offered. Sometimes, there is a discount for seniors.

Here are some places to look for support for your art supplies and instruction:

- Art/craft store classes
- Home repair stores
- Online classes or demonstrations
- Park/rec centers
- Colleges
- Museums
- Sewing and fabric stores
- DVDs
- Books
- Clubs/groups
- Local art societies
- Specialized pottery making stores

- Leather work supply stores   •   Garden centers

Allowing your creative side to emerge is one of the great gifts of retirement. We are not graded, and our projects serve to allow our full self to come into being. For many people, the process of creating generates a feeling of "flow" or of being in harmony. Let yourself experience the fun and the learning that is the artistic process.

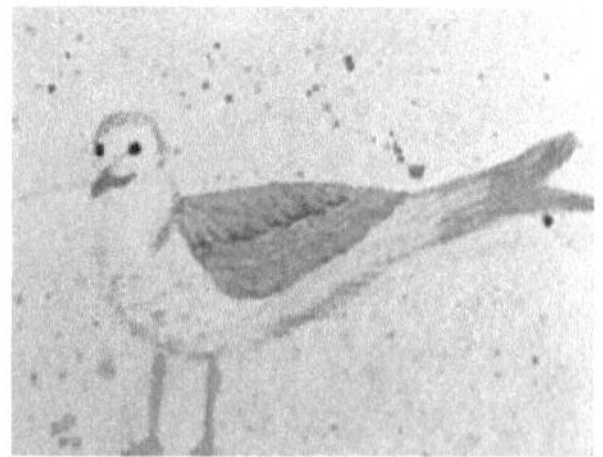

Learning to watercolor is fun!

6 CULINARY ARTS

You may not think of yourself as a chef, but there are many creative ways to engage with the food we eat, and the beverages we drink.

Years ago, the movie Julie & Julia, portrayed a young woman cooking her way through Julia Child's *The Way To Cook*. While that is certainly one way to learn new techniques and recipes, there are other options.

Local recreation centers and parks and colleges offer courses that specialize in the cuisine of a country or region, or in a technique. These are a good way to get some expert guidance in learning a new way to prepare food. For instance, I took a bread making class with a friend, which was both educational and fun. My son took a sushi preparation course. The range of courses is wide – see if you can find one you would enjoy.

For healthy eating, many hospitals and medical centers offer courses for cooking for diabetics or healthier meal planning.

A friend's husband is a competitive BBQ chef – traveling around the region to compete in BBQ cook offs. Hobbies like this allow us to pursue an interest, and make friends in the community.

Some of you may be interested in trying your hand at creating beers or wines at home. There are a number of books, online videos and courses available to teach the skills needed to begin brewing your own beverages.

Another option: cheese making. Simple cheeses can be made at home with very little equipment and simple recipes. You may be surprised at how delicious your cheeses turn out!

Fermented foods, from pickles to yogurts to kimchi, are another way to add to your cooking repertoire. Books and videos are available to guide you.

Creating new dishes or beverages, and learning new processes, can be an enjoyable pastime, and can help improve your health, by incorporating new ingredients and dishes.

7 READING AND WRITING

Having time to sit and read is a great pleasure. New books and audio books are available at your library. If you prefer to own your own books, thrift stores, "friends of the library" sales, and garage sales offer low prices and some interesting selections.

There may be discussion groups and book clubs sponsored by your local library, or available online, through MeetUp, NextDoor or other resources. Deeper engagement with the reading material and making new friends are both benefits of joining a book club.

Reading to others is a gift to yourself and the audience. Reading to kids at schools or libraries enhances their learning. My local library enlists volunteers to read to kids, to help keep them interested in books, and improve their reading skills. Reading to those hospitalized or in nursing homes is a kindness, and is a great way to share your love of reading.

Writing is a wonderful endeavor. There are worlds you can create – poems that reflect what you see; short stories; a family history; a novel; a blog or a journal of your life. Consider finding a local writers club if getting started seems hard. Many colleges and rec centers offer course in getting started with a writing project. There are also online writers groups that review each other's work and encourage each other.

If you have a special skill or knowledge, a book may be a great project. A friend wrote a book on a card game, codifying its rules, and adding some social commentary on the game. Another friend has written several romance novels. Both of these authors use the "print on demand" method of selling books, instead of a having publisher and having inventory.

You can begin with simple writing notes in an inexpensive notebook, and see where it talks you. A few minutes each morning may become your cookbook, poetry collection or a gripping spy novel. Just let yourself write, with no judgement. You may emerge as an author.

8 VOLUNTEERING

The opportunities to volunteer are amazing in their variety. Studies have shown that people who volunteer are happier and healthier than those who do not. There are many ways you can contribute, even if your health isn't perfect, or your mobility is limited.

You can look at where your charitable contributions have been going, to see if the organizations you have been supporting financially would also benefit from your time and efforts. Here are just a few ideas to get you started:

Schools need helpers who can read to kids, and tutor in many subjects, supervise after school activities and organize events. School and community sports teams often need coaches, umpires, drivers for team meets, and other adults to help support the team practices and games.

Parks and Recreations Centers need information desk help, interpretive guides, weed pullers, trail guides, and activity leaders.

Emergency services, from Red Cross to your local fire department, need a wide range of skills are to help with everything from first aid to fund raising to operating radios in a disaster.

Community support groups, like Habitat for Humanity, need builders (they teach you the needed skills), and Re-store personnel; community food closets need help with inventory and distribution, stocking shelves and helping clients. In many states, children in the social services process will have an appointed volunteer advocate to help represent the child's interests. I volunteer with a local Habitat for Humanity team, and have learned practical skills while meeting a lot of interesting new people. It is very rewarding to work with the new homeowners as we build together, and meet the families that are now able to buy an affordable home.

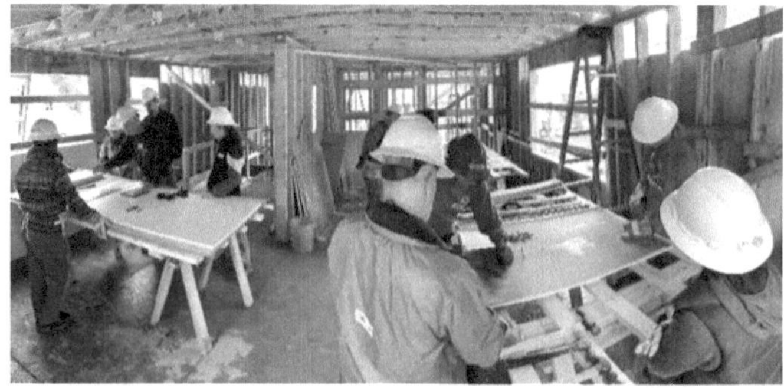

Working on a new Habitat home is very rewarding

Animal support groups and shelters need help socializing animals, accompanying animals to adoption events and grooming animals. My sister creates social media attention for animals that need to be adopted, and "hosts" the adoption events for cats at a local pet store.

Services for the elderly include Meals on Wheels, which needs drivers, groups that support companion animals brought to nursing home brighten residents' days, and medical appointment drivers are needed for those who can no longer drive.

Environmental and outdoors groups, like Keep America Beautiful use volunteers for cleanups and office work. Nature Conservancy had opportunities to help maintain reserves and observe wildlife for scientific research. The Appalachian Trail Conservancy and Pacific Crest Trail Association both use volunteers to maintain trails and shelters, as well as help with outreach activities. Cornell University and Audubon Society use citizen scientists to perform surveys, including surveying birds right in your backyard. For many years, my father acted as a water quality monitor for a lake, sampling water to help make sure it was safe for swimming.

The National Weather Service trains people and uses data from citizen observers to create better local forecasts, with more precise data. Their training is called SkyWarn, and may be offered near you.

Hospitals and nursing homes need volunteers for everything from helping families whose member is in surgery, to helping patients eat, to playing games with children who are hospitalized. Hospice care groups benefit from volunteers that help the families of the patient, or provide comfort in other ways, such as playing soothing music or providing visitors with refreshments.

Museums, theatres and botanic gardens need volunteers to lead talks, operate gift stores and greet the public. My brother-in-law volunteers at an aircraft museum, and helps with the restoration of old airplanes. There are needs for every imaginable skill at museums, historic homes and sites across the country.

Mentors are always needed for small businesses and for aspiring farmers. SCORE volunteers help small business owners plan and manage their businesses. Your expertise could help a new business owner launch their dream.

There are many service organizations supporting veterans or active duty military. The United Service Organization (USO), American Legion, and the Veterans of Foreign Wars of the United States are just a few. If you are former military, or wish to support our active duty troops, these organizations can help you make a difference.

There are many civic groups, with missions to help children, or build stronger communities. Moose Lodge, Kiwanis International, and Rotary International are a few examples, and have groups in many cities and towns across the country.

Political campaigns always need volunteers. From writing postcards to get out the vote, to canvassing neighborhoods, to helping set up town hall meetings, candidates always need help. Supporting a candidate that you believe will improve your community or state or country is a worthwhile endeavor. The people who represent us on school boards and state legislatures matter, and you can help make sure that good candidates are elected. This is another way to meet new, like-minded friends, and to interact with other members of your community.

Your city or county may have a volunteer coordinating website. Volunteer.Gov has a wide selection, including opportunities at our National Parks. You will be amazed at the variety of opportunities and needs.

For the adventure minded, the Peace Corps (Peace Corps.Gov) has needs around the world for people willing to travel and live in another country.

If you belong to a faith group, there are likely activities from visiting ill congregation members to teaching children to singing that all need volunteers.

It is very rewarding to know you have contributed to making the world a little better place by your actions. As a bonus, you may make new friends with like-minded people!

9 LEARNING

This is the time to learn a new skill, or pursue and interest in a topic you like.

Have you always wanted to learn a new language? Your library has books and CDs and DVDs. Your local college or park service may offer classes. There are informal "conversational" language clubs and online lessons. You can learn can new language and culture!

Wish you knew more about fossils or rocks? In addition to local colleges, your local museum may offer classes or workshops. There may be a fossil or "rock hound" club in your area, where you can learn from others. Online clubs exist, too, and offer discussions and lectures.

Many county extension services offer "Master Gardener" or "Master Naturalist" courses. You can learn about our amazing planet, and the plants and animals that inhabit it. These programs usually include some "giving back" time, where you help members of your community with planning what to plant, diagnosing a plant disease, identifying wildlife or other topics. A great way to both learn and contribute!

Check out the classes at your local parks, rec centers, senior centers, garden nurseries and libraries. From bonsai to woodworking, there are classes or clubs that can expand your skills and knowledge, while adding new friends to your life.

Kahn Academy (KahnAcademy.Org) provides free, online classes to anyone. MIT OpenCourseWare is an online resource for all the MIT course content. Your local colleges and university may also offer free online or in-person (audit) of classes.

A friend has recently taken up the clarinet, which she played as a child. Working with a good teacher, she is playing music and enjoying the challenge of working with her instrument in new ways.

You may read this elsewhere, but I'll repeat it: One of the best ways to retain your memory and cognitive skills is by learning something new. So pick up a new interest (beekeeping, anyone?) or dust off an old one, and get started!

10 GAMES

Playing games helps keep our brains sharp, and can bring new friends into our lives.

Many communities have bridge clubs, or bunco clubs. There are often classes, as well, to teach new players the rules of bridge, poker or other card games.

Checkers and chess offer a chance to use strategy and long range planning, as well as friendly competition. Community centers may have group playing times available.

Board games communities often have a weekly meeting time to play. Try looking in your community to find a group, or start a group.

Libraries may have information about community gatherings, MeetUp.com or NextDoor.com may have information about game groups in your neighborhood.

11 TRAVEL

The freedom to travel is one of the traditional things people look forward to in their retirement. Maybe you have a "bucket list" of places you'd like to see. In addition to the traditional cruises and tour companies, there are other options available to you.

Turin, Italy – churches, castles and museums

Road Scholar is a not-for-profit educational travel service that specializes in trips for older adults. Some trips are designed for grandchildren to participate as well.

If you are attracted to the RV life, you can rent one first, before committing to an expensive machine. These require more maintenance than some people realize, so look before you leap. Renting an RV is a good way to see if it is right for you. RVs can provide you with a "home away from home" that allows you to travel and see the country.

Parks and campgrounds often rent cabins or tents on platforms at reasonable rates, allowing you to enjoy nature and new location.

Amazing Alaska is a wonderful travel destination

International Home Exchange (IHEN.com) lets you swap houses to stay in another location, or list your home for a vacation rental while you are away.

Some volunteer jobs at a preserve or park may offer accommodations, or a spot for your RV or camper.

"Staycations", where you explore your own local area are an inexpensive way to see new things. Your state tourism bureau will have maps and information you can use to find places nearby. Have you visited all the local museums and historic homes? Been to every park in a two hour radius? Gone to the botanic garden? Checked out the plays and recitals at your local colleges? Try looking at your home through the eyes of a tour guide. Are there wineries to visit? Organic farms that give tours or offer "you pick" days? Historic churches you'd like to see? Is there an historical society that has mapped important places? You may be surprised to find how many interesting places are within an easy drive of your home. Pack up a picnic lunch and explore!

Some charities, like Habitat for Humanity International, offer opportunities to give back overseas. You may provide airfare, and the charity may provide housing and meals. You will get to experience local people and cultures in a new way. I recently attended a talk given by a beekeeper who travels with a group to Malawi, to exchange beekeeping ideas and knowledge with Malawian beekeepers.

From exploring your own locale to traveling the world, allow yourself to enjoy seeing new things and meeting new people. Planning a trip is half the fun. Your local library and the Internet have information about parks, cities and countries around the world. Take the time to enjoy the "pre-journey", and find the places or activities that most interest you. For example, I am planning a trip to Yellowstone and Grand Teton with my sister and her husband. To help with costs, we'll rent a cabin, and stock it with food to make many of our meals. Using Frommer's guide book and the Internet, I've scheduled a float trip on the Snake River, several days of trail walks near geysers and lakes and waterfalls and glaciers, and a horseback trail ride. We'll use our lifetime Senior Pass from the National Park Service to access the parks. We'll hunt fossils in Kemmerer, Wyoming on our way back to Salt Lake City (much less expensive flights than those close to the parks). Using your imagination, and looking for options can make trips more affordable, as well as more fun!

12 MUSIC

Almost everyone enjoys some aspect of music – whether creating it, or listening to it. Like reading, you now have time to bring more music into your life.

If you enjoy listening to music, in addition to concert venues, your community may have opportunities to hear local school bands or orchestras for little or no cost, enjoy summer outdoor concerts by local bands, listen to military bands and orchestras, or hear recitals at churches or other religious institutions. Colleges may offer low cost or free access to dress rehearsals for their orchestras or bands. I once heard the wonderful Air Force String Quartet for free, when they played in a local church. Look around, and see what appears!

Libraries often have some musical education materials – Great Courses or others, that allow you to learn the intricacies of music, and appreciate it more deeply.

If you have always wanted to learn to play an instrument, there are books, DVDs, and online classes to help you. Music stores offer lessons, and you might find a music major college student willing to teach you for a reasonable fee. Secondhand instruments are widely available (Craigslist, eBay, NextDoor) and might be a good place to start, without spending a bundle. Music stores offer rentals, as well.

And don't forget your built-in instrument, your voice! Singing classes are offered through park services, or local colleges. Your faith group may have a choir, and a director willing to help you learn to sing.

If you played or sang earlier in life, you may be able to find an adult group to join – a community orchestra, a barbershop singing group, or a local music venue that has jam sessions. Or you can start one!

Retirement is the perfect time to allow yourself to explore singing, or listening, or playing an instrument. Enjoy the process, and let yourself unleash your inner musician.

13 FRIENDS AND FAMILY

One of the great pleasures of retirement is that you have time to meet and make new friends. As you pursue your interests, you will meet like-minded people. This is a great time to invite someone to meet you for coffee, or go to lunch, or plan an activity that is aligned with your common interests.

In addition to service groups mentioned in the volunteer section, there are an abundance of clubs that are focused on different interests. Garden clubs are a great way to learn about gardening and landscaping. Bridge clubs can sharpen your card playing skills, and give you new companions. There are Men's Shed clubs around the world that create a space for men to get together, share tools, make projects and have companionship. Rock hounds and fossil hunters can find kindred spirits and knowledgeable friends in clubs and societies focused in these areas. Photography clubs can help you improve your skills, and make friends as you have outings to gardens or rivers or other photo shoot locations.

Say "yes" to new experiences — concerts or adventures that you learn about, and invite a friend, old or new, to join you. One of the best pieces of advice was one I got shortly before retirement from a friend who had recently retired. His advice "just say "YES"", has encouraged me to do new things, and to enjoy the process of learning what best suits me in retirement.

Don't overlook the companionship that comes from a pet. A

number of studies have shown that dog owners walk more, and enjoy health benefits from having dogs. Caring for your pet, and having a companion are good for our mental health, too. If pet ownership isn't possible, local shelters and rescue organizations always need volunteers.

Junior surveys his kingdom

Visiting family and friends, or having them visit you, may be easier now that your schedule is more flexible.

Make time to see old friends, and enjoy the bonds of friendship. I recently hosted a group of people who worked together almost twenty years ago for an afternoon get together. It was wonderful to see everyone re-connect, and catch up.

Find ways to spend time with friends and enjoy yourself!

14 SIDE BUSINESSES/PART TIME WORK

First, your current job may have options to go part time to ease into retirement. If you choose this method, please start a new activity or two from this guide to start your journey, creating new routines and opening new vistas.

Maybe you have always had a "side hustle" or part time work. If not, you may find that having a flexible job, or money-making hobby, fits nicely into your new life.

If you are artistic, you may want to investigate local craft fairs or Etsy, as means to sell your bird houses, jewelry or other items you create.

If you have a skill, there are a lot of opportunities to teach others. For example, park/rec centers classes offer classes on Bonsai, playing bridge, making pasta, building birdhouses, etc. Or if you have a computer skill, you could teach that to others.

If you enjoy animals, dog walking might be a good part time job for you. Or animal sitting at your home, or in other people's homes.

House sitting, especially in an area that you'd like to visit, might be a perfect way to see a new place inexpensively.

The "gig" economy offers options ranging from Uber/Lyft driving to Task Rabbit (any task) that can bring income and keep you busy.

One of the great blessings of retirement for me is that I can teach a couple of yoga classes during the week, not just once a week on a weekend. And I've had time to create, plan and execute a week-long yoga retreats for beginners in Tulum, Mexico, sharing my love of yoga with others in a beautiful location.

One friend, retired from government, is working toward a Master Sommelier designation – taking classes to learn about wine regions, and working part time in a winery. She loves it!

If you've always wanted to work in a bookstore, now might be your time. Or help folks select the right plants in a garden center. Or dispense advice on the right parts/tools in a hardware store. Or be a lifeguard.

Finding a part time job that is fun and interesting is possible!

15 SPIRITUAL GROWTH

As our lives change focus from work and career to a "whole life" vision, many of us feel the calling to spiritual matters.

For those who are members of a faith, this may be a time to explore the texts of your faith in a new way, perhaps with a study group. Many faiths offer prayer retreats or silent retreats in which you have time to reconnect to the tenets of your faith. Not far from my home is a monastery that offers silent prayer weekends for non-clergy.

For those who are not aligned with a specific faith, spiritual growth may be created through participating in ethics groups, or meditations on life and its meaning, or connecting with our beautiful planet and its people.

Finding meaning in life is a life long journey. For some, reading religious texts for the writing of devout practitioners help create a path for growth. There are scholarly works, such as the "Great Courses" series (often available through libraries) that can illuminate the essential teachings and the path that a faith has taken over time.

For some, acting in charity or service, feeding the homeless, caring for those in hospice, or rebuilding homes destroyed by hurricanes can become a way to move closer to their spiritual path.

Sitting in quiet meditation or prayer for a few minutes each day can help us with both clarity of purpose and peace of mind. Meditation is not complicated, and can be done anywhere. Sitting quietly, we can focus on our breathing, or on a word or phrase. If the mind wanders off, just gently bring it back to your breath or your word or phrase.

A simple practice of gratitude, reflecting on the goodness in our life, the beauty of a garden or the appreciation of a kind act, is a spiritual practice that helps us enjoy our life. A gratitude journal, created by noting just a few things you are grateful for each day, can improve your appreciation of the many blessings in our lives.

16 CREATING A NEW ROUTINE

One of the things I hear from people is "I don't know what I'll do all day!". If that sounds like you, here are some suggestions to get you started on your new life:

Create a flexible schedule for yourself that includes a physical activity, like a walk or a swim, at least three days of your week. A walking group or walking buddy can help keep you motivated and keep you moving. For some of us, attending a scheduled class at a rec center or gym keeps us on schedule. One friend who retired recently goes to the gym every morning at nine, keeping active and becoming more fit.

Find your volunteer opportunity, and schedule yourself to volunteer once a week, or more. If you find several things you are interested in, try them out. I volunteer at a local park to help manage invasive plants, which lets me also enjoy the beautiful river, and see the eagles raise their young. I volunteer for Habitat for Humanity, and have learned skills ranging from drywall hanging to making a gate for a fence. I also volunteer for our county Community Emergency Response Team, helping with disaster preparation drills.

And now, what about fun? Garden club? Pottery class? Cooking every recipe in the Julia Child cookbook? Senior soccer team? Finally learning to tango? Watercolor workshop? Add something fun to your schedule and let yourself simply enjoy it.

Schedule some "planning" time. Use this time to explore what learning or skills or arts or writing or other activity you'd like to do. Writing a couple of pages in a journal every morning can help with seeing your life more clearly, and help with ideas and planning. Your morning journal can be the place where mundane thoughts are recorded, or emotions are released, and creative ideas are allowed to take form. Planning time can be a weekly activity, too – planning a vacation or your next endeavor.

And don't forget to savor the precious time you have to enjoy your morning coffee without rushing out the door.

Layer these activities on your calendar, and get started creating your new life!

17 RESOURCES

Here are some places to look for additional ideas and information:

Libraries

MeetUp

NextDoor

Online "how to" videos and classes

WikiHow

Local colleges

Local recreation centers and parks

County/City/National Volunteer offices

All Non-Profits

AARP

Kahn Academy

Museums

Botanical gardens

County extension services

ABOUT THE AUTHOR

Dona Dickinson is enjoying her retirement, and hopes this small book will help you create your perfect retirement.
In addition to her volunteer activities, she teaches yoga and leads a yearly yoga and meditation retreat.
She lives in Great Falls, Virginia with her husband, Richard, along with dogs, cats, goats, chickens and bees.

www.ingramcontent.com/pod-product-compliance
Lightning Source LLC
Chambersburg PA
CBHW051130250726
48655CB00007B/2987